SCIENCE

KEY STAGE 2   LEVELS 3–5
TEST A

To do this test you will need a **pencil**,
a **ruler**, a **rubber** and a **watch** or
clock to time yourself.

Sit at a table in a quiet place.

Page	M	
2–3		
4–5	6	
6–7	7	
8–9	9	
10–11	8	
12–13	6	
14–15	5	
16	3	
Total	50	

GH01184908

> Ask an adult to read through the test instructions with you before you start.

INSTRUCTIONS

1. You will have **45 minutes** to do this test.

2. Read all the words in each question carefully.

3. If you cannot read a word ask an adult to tell you what it says.

4. Use any diagrams or pictures to help you.

5. Try to explain your answers accurately if you are asked to do so.

6. Do not worry if you do not finish all the questions. Do as many as you can.

7. Do not waste time on a question you cannot do. Move quickly on to the next one.

8. Read instructions carefully and write your answers in the spaces highlighted by
   the handwriting symbols.

9. Move straight on from one page to the next without waiting to be told.

10. If there is time left when you have finished, check your answers and try to do any
    questions you missed out earlier.

Your first name	
Your last name	

Parents and teachers: Removable instructions and answers are in the centre of the book.

Earth, sun and moon

1 The earth, the sun and the moon are all shaped like spheres but their sizes differ.

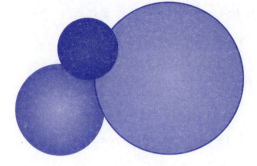

a. Write their names in the correct order of size starting with the biggest.

_____

b. Complete the following sentences by choosing the correct word from the circle at the bottom of the page.

i   The sun is a _____.

ii The earth is a _____.

iii The moon is a _____ of the Earth.

iv The sun is at the centre of our _____ system.

(force, satellite, star, solar, process, seed, planet, mineral)

Test A

Life processes

2 Look at the drawings of these six living things.

blossom

frog

pelican

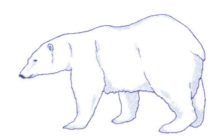
polar bear

trout

pine tree

Which THREE things do all the living things shown here do?

Tick THREE boxes.

grow	☐	fly	☐
jump	☐	feed	☐
reproduce	☐	swim	☐

Q2

3 marks

Test A

3

Total

Comparing materials

3 Some materials are natural but others have to be made.

a. Tick the materials that are natural.

glass	☐	water	☐
wood	☐	cardboard	☐
plastic	☐	stone	☐

b. Write the names of TWO other **natural** materials.

_____

Not all materials look and feel the same.
Look at the objects illustrated below.

c. Tick the objects made from a **smooth** material.

   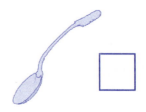

Test A

4

d. Write the words in the correct column on the table.

concrete brick   wooden door   metal wire

rubber hose-pipe   steel girder   plastic ruler

will bend	will not bend

Light

 4 Colin and Helen investigate which materials allow light to pass through. They hold different materials below a bright table lamp to see which materials let the light pass through.

Complete the table below to predict their results.

Tick ONE box in each row.
The first one has been done for you.

	some light passes through	no light passes through
clear glass	✓	
aluminium foil		
tissue paper		
cardboard		
black plastic bag		
frosted glass		

Test A   5   Total

Plant growth and nutrition

5 Two squares of plastic sheeting were pegged out on healthy grass for a week.
One of the plastic sheets was black and the other was clear.

a. Why was the grass yellow where the black plastic had been?

_____

_____

Q5a

1 mark

Animals take in their food but plants do not.

b. How do plants get their food?

_____

_____

Q5b

1 mark

c. Which of these sentences are **true**?

Tick THREE boxes.

The roots of a plant grow towards darkness. ☐

The roots anchor the plant. ☐

The roots of a plant support the flowers. ☐

Plant roots get rid of unwanted food. ☐

The roots of a plant take in water. ☐

Q5c

2 marks

Test A

6

Water cycle

6 The water cycle is the movement of water around the Earth. It has been going on for millions of years.

The water cycle

Copy these sentences in the correct order to show what is happening in the diagram. Label each sentence A, B, C or D.

Clouds cool to form water, which falls as rain.

The wind blows clouds over the land.

Heat from the Sun evaporates water from the sea to form clouds.

Rainwater flows in rivers and streams to the sea.

_____

_____

_____

_____

Test A

Q6

3 marks

Total

Earth and space

7 a. How long does it take the earth to rotate once on its axis?

Q7a

1 mar

b. Complete this diagram to show why it is light in some parts of the world when it is dark in others.

Earth

Sun

Q7b

1 mar

c. How many days are there in a leap year?

Tick ONE box.

365 ☐   536 ☐   603 ☐   366 ☐

Q7c

1 mar

1996 was a leap year.

d. Write the next four years that are leap years.

Q7d

_____   _____   _____   _____

1 mar

Test A

8

Skeleton and muscles

8 The human skeleton has 206 bones. It forms an important framework on which to attach muscles.

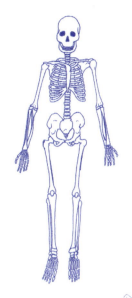

a. Name TWO other ways in which the skeleton is important to humans.

i _____

ii _____

b. Which part of the skeleton protects the brain?

   _____

c. What advantage is it to humans to have some of their bones hollow?

_____

d. Complete the sentence below. Choose the best word from those in the box.

Muscles make it possible for your body to _____

| sleep | grow | move | feel | stand |

Test A   9   Total

Heat insulation

 Mark and Lisa set up the experiment shown in the diagram. They want to find out which is the better heat insulator: cotton wool or plastic foam.
Their teacher looks at the test and says, "This is not a fair test."

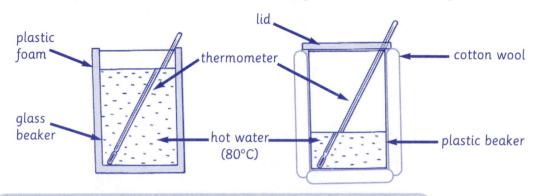

Write down TWO reasons why the test is not fair.

_____

_____

Forces

 a. What force makes the leaves from a tree fall to the ground?

_____

b. Tick **true** or **false**.

There are no forces acting upon an object that is perfectly still.

true ☐   false ☐

c. Circle the name of the THREE surfaces listed below that will have the most friction.

shiny   smooth   bumpy   rough   wet   dry

Test A

Adaptation

11 A plant or animal has special features that allow it to survive in the habitat where it lives.

a. Link each animal to its habitat.

b. Choose the correct word to write in each space.

Eagles have a _____ which helps them rip their food.

Squirrels have _____ that crack open nuts.

Otters have a _____ which helps them swim quickly.

(teeth   feathers   eyes   tail   beak   fur)

c. Write ONE way in which this fish is adapted to its life in water.

 _____

States of matter

12 Everything is either a solid, a liquid or a gas.

a. Connect words from each block to form a sentence. One has been done for you.

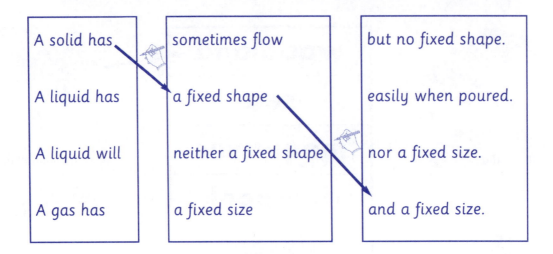

A solid has	sometimes flow	but no fixed shape.
A liquid has	a fixed shape	easily when poured.
A liquid will	neither a fixed shape	nor a fixed size.
A gas has	a fixed size	and a fixed size.

b. Tick either **solid**, **liquid** or **gas**.

	solid	liquid	gas
wood			
oxygen			
oil			
paper			

	solid	liquid	gas
air			
petrol			
milk			
iron			

c. Some solid foods melt easily when heated by the sun.

Write the names of THREE of them.

_____

Test A

The blood system

13 a. Put a tick in the correct box to show the position of this person's heart.

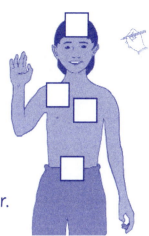

b. Blood flows faster when the heart pumps faster.

i Which TWO of the following activities makes the heart pump faster?

 skipping ☐   reading ☐

eating ☐   running ☐

When the heart pumps blood faster, we also breathe faster.

ii Why is this so?

_____

c. Choose the correct words to write in each space.

 The tubes that carry blood from your heart are called _____ .

 _____ carry blood back to the heart.

| veins | lungs | nerves | arteries | canals |

Test A

13

Total

Electrical circuits

 14 You are going to make a simple electrical circuit that will switch a bulb on and off.

a. Make a list of the things you will need to carry out the task.

_____

_____

_____

Q14a

1 mark

b. Draw a labelled circuit diagram to show how you will connect together all the items listed in part a.
Remember, you must be able to switch the bulb on and off. Use the correct circuit symbols in your diagram.

Q14b

1 mark

Test A

c. You discover that the circuit you have made does not light up the bulb.

> Write down TWO possible reasons why the bulb does not light up.

i _____

ii _____

2 marks

d. Steel is an electrical conductor.
If steel wire is coiled into a long spring it can be used to alter the electrical current in a circuit.

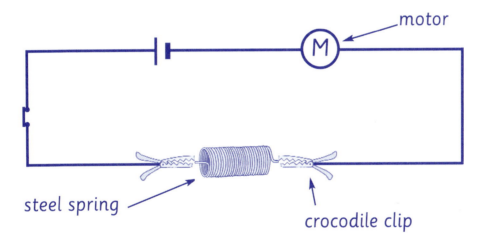

> Look where the crocodile clips are attached in the diagram. If you moved the clips closer to each other, what would happen to the motor?

Tick ONE box.

It would run faster. ☐

It would run more slowly. ☐

It would stay the same. ☐

1 mark

Separating materials

a. Connect this sentence beginning, with its correct ending.

         ...separate one liquid from another.

We filter things to...   ...make liquids thinner.

...separate a solid from a liquid.

Sue and Keith put their family's washing outside to dry.

b. Write in the correct word to complete this sentence.

Wet washing hanging outside dries because the water

_____ .

c. What sort of weather will make the washing dry quickly?

_____

STOP HERE

Test A

Have a go! Science Tests

Ages 10–11

Pull-out instructions and answers

Contents

Introduction for Parents ii

Answers to Test A iii

Answers to Test B v

Working Out Your Child's National Curriculum Level vii

Vocabulary Your Child Should Know vii

Key Vocabulary viii

Tests A and B can be found in the main body of the book.

SCIENCE Practice for
Key Stage 2 National Tests
(Levels 3–5)

Pull-out instructions and answers

Introduction for Parents

These practice tests have been compiled to help your child prepare for the National Tests in Science that are taken towards the end of Year 6 at Primary School. The layout of the test material, the marking scheme and the level thresholds closely resemble the 'real' test papers. This means that it is possible, by using **Tests A** and **B**, to gain an indication of the National Curriculum level at which your child is working.

Your child should do **Test A** first and then **Test B**.

- ❖ Do each test on a separate day.
- ❖ Choose a time of day when your child is not tired or irritable.
- ❖ Be positive and cheerful before your child begins and give as much encouragement as you can so that they start each test with confidence.
- ❖ Make sure that there are no disturbances while the test is being taken.
- ❖ Go through the instructions on the front page of each test thoroughly with your child before they begin.
- ❖ Answer any questions or queries your child might have about the test instructions.
- ❖ During the test, if your child cannot read a word, you may read it out to them but do not explain its meaning.
- ❖ Make sure your child has a pencil, a ruler, a rubber and a clock or watch to time themselves.
- ❖ Once started, don't fuss and keep looking over your child's shoulder or distract them in any way.

Marking the tests

- ❖ Use the mark schemes provided on pages iii-vi of this booklet and award marks as indicated in the scheme. Use your discretion when marking as some answers may have more than one correct response.
- ❖ In the margin of each test paper, alongside each question, there is a mark box for each question part. In this box write the number of marks scored by you child for that part of the question. If your child gets the question wrong place a '0' in the box. If your child does not attempt the question put a '–' in the box. Do not leave any mark box empty.
- ❖ At the bottom of all right-hand page margins and on the final page of each test is a 'total' box. Fill this in with either the total number of marks scored on the double page spread or, in the case of the last page for each test, the total number of marks for that page. Write each of these totals on the 'marking grid' on the front cover of each test, add them up and fill in the total marks scored in the appropriate space.
- ❖ Transfer this final mark to the correct test column on the first table on page vii of this booklet.

The questions in both Test A and B cover the NC level ranges 3–5.

After you have marked both tests follow the instructions on page vii of this booklet to work out your child's National Curriculum Level. Remember, these are only practice tests and the results obtained by your child should be interpreted as guidance only.

Have a go! Science Tests Ages 10–11

Pull-out instructions and answers

Answers to Test A

Q			Marks
1	a.	sun, earth, moon	1
	b.	Award 1 mark for two sections or 2 marks for all sections correct.	2
	i	star	
	ii	planet	
	iii	satellite	
	iv	solar	
		Do not credit the second mark if only three sections are correct.	

2 Award 1 mark for each of: — **3**

grow	✓	fly	☐
jump	☐	feed	✓
reproduce	✓	swim	☐

If more than three boxes are ticked, deduct 1 mark for each incorrect answer.

3

a. Award 1 mark if all three boxes ticked correctly. — **1**

glass	☐	water	✓
wood	✓	cardboard	☐
plastic	☐	stone	✓

b. Award 1 mark for two natural materials such as: — **1**
coal, wool, leather, cork, bone, feather etc.

c. Award 1 mark if all three boxes are ticked correctly. — **1**

d. Award 1 mark if all six materials are in the correct column on the table. — **1**

will bend	will not bend
metal wire	concrete brick
rubber hose-pipe	wooden door
plastic ruler	steel girder

4 Award 2 marks for the correct classification of all five. — **2**

	some light passes through	no light passes through
clear glass	✓	
aluminium foil		✓
tissue paper	✓	
cardboard		✓
black plastic bag		✓
frosted glass	✓	

Award 1 mark for any three or four correctly classified.

Q			Marks
5	a.	Award 1 mark for any of these responses: it (the grass) had no light/sunlight it (the grass) had no chlorophyll photosynthesis could not take place	1
	b.	Award 1 mark for any of these responses: they (plants) make it they (plants) absorb energy from sunlight they (plants) photosynthesise	1
	c.	Award 2 marks for all three boxes correctly ticked. Award 1 mark for two correctly ticked boxes out of three or just two correctly ticked boxes.	2

The roots of a plant grow towards darkness.	✓
The roots anchor the plant.	✓
The roots of a plant support the flowers.	☐
Plant roots get rid of unwanted food.	☐
The roots of a plant take in water.	✓

Give no credit if four or more boxes are ticked.

6 Award 3 marks if each sentence is in the correct order and matched to the correct letter: — **3**
A. Heat from the sun evaporates water from the sea to form clouds.
B. The wind blows clouds over the land.
C. Clouds cool to form water which falls as rain.
D. Rainwater flows in rivers and streams to the sea.
Award 2 marks if all sentences are matched to the correct letter but not in the correct order.

7

a. Accept: — **1**
24 hours/one day/a day/about 24 hours
Do not give credit for a response with no units indicated.

b. Award 1 mark for a completed diagram along the lines shown below. — **1**

far side of the Earth in shadow — **Earth** — light rays — **Sun**

Do not give credit for a diagram that does not have the far side of the earth in shadow.

c. 365 ☐ 536 ☐ 603 ☐ 366 ✓ — **1**

Do not give credit if more than one box is ticked.

d. 2000, 2004, 2008, 2012 (in any order) — **1**

8

a. i Award 1 mark for a description of **support**: — **1**
if provides support/keeps you a solid shape/prevents you from collapse/keeps you rigid/helps you stand.

ii Award 1 mark for a description of **movement**: — **1**
it helps you to move/run/walk/swim/balance

Do not give credit more than once for responses in either of the categories listed above.
(You can also award 1 mark for an answer such as: it protects your internal organs/it makes blood - instead of an answer from the two categories above.)

Pull-out instructions and answers

Q			Marks
	b.	skull/cranium	1
	c.	it makes the skeleton lighter in weight	1
	d.	muscles make it possible for your body to move.	1
9		Award 1 mark each for any two of the following three reasons to a maximum of 2 marks: The containers are made of different materials. The containers do not contain the same amounts of water. One container has a lid but the other container does not have a lid.	2
10	a.	gravity	1
	b.	Ticked: false	1
	c.	Circled: bumpy, rough, dry Do not credit the mark if more than three words are circled.	1
11	a.	Award 1 mark if all five animals are correctly connected to their habitat.	1
	b.	Award 1 mark if all three sentences are correct. Eagles have a **beak** which helps them rip their food. Squirrels have **teeth** that can crack open nuts. Otters have a **tail** which helps them to swim quickly.	1
	c.	Award 1 mark for any of the following adaptations: it has fins it is a streamline shape it has gills	1
12	a.	Award 1 mark for three correctly connected sentences: A solid had a fixed shape and a fixed size. A liquid has a fixed size but no fixed shape. A liquid will sometimes flow easily when poured. A gas has neither a fixed shape nor a fixed size.	1
	b.	Award 1 mark for all materials correctly identified.	1

	solid	liquid	gas
wood	✓		
oxygen			✓
oil		✓	
paper	✓		

	solid	liquid	gas
air			✓
petrol		✓	
milk		✓	
iron	✓		

Q			Marks
	c.	Award 1 mark for any three food items that melt easily when heated by the sun, e.g. butter, margarine, lard, chocolate, cheese, sugary sweets etc.	1

Q			Marks
13	a.		1
	b.	Award 1 mark if both section i and ii are answered correctly.	1
	i	skipping ✓ reading ☐ eating ☐ running ✓	
	ii	When the heart pumps blood faster, we also breathe faster because the body needs to take more **oxygen** into the lungs. Do not credit a mark if only section i or section ii is correct. The answer to section ii is incorrect if it does not contain the word **oxygen**.	
	c.	Award 1 mark if both sentences are correct. The tubes that carry blood from your heart are called **arteries**. Veins carry blood back to your heart.	1
14	a.	Award 1 mark for: cell (battery), bulb (bulb holder), wire (copper, steel), switch	1
	b.	Award 1 mark for a labelled circuit diagram showing all the items in any order on the circuit.	1
	c.	Award 1 mark each for any two of the following reasons to a maximum of 2 marks: The cell (battery) is flat/dead/broken/faulty The bulb is broken/blown/faulty The switch is broken/faulty The circuit is not complete/there is a break in the circuit	2
	d.	It would run faster. ✓ It would run more slowly. ☐ It would stay the same. ☐ Do not give credit if more than one box is ticked.	1
15	a.	We filter things to - separate a solid from a liquid.	1
	b.	evaporates	1
	c.	warm (hot), windy weather Credit the mark if either of the above weather conditions are indicated.	1

Have a go! Science Tests   Ages 10–11

Answers to Test B

Q			Marks
1	a.	Award 2 marks for a correct description of what each type of tooth does: i cut/chisel/slice/chop/nibble food ii crunch/grind/crush/chew/mash/smash food iii rip/tear/grip/hold food Award 1 mark for any two correct descriptions.	2
	b.	Award 1 mark for: eating less sugar ✓ drinking lots of water ☐ visiting the dentist regularly ✓ eating less fat ☐ Do not give credit if more than two boxes are ticked.	1
2	a.	bronze, copper, steel	1
	b.	the material being tested is not an electrical conductor	1
	c.	TRUE	1
3	a.	15cm (also credit either 14cm or 16cm)	1
	b.	70cm	1
	c.	opaque	1
4		C(1) A(2) B(3)	1, 1, 1
5	a.	☐ ☐ ☐ ✓ (sieve) Do not give credit if more than one box is ticked.	1
	b.	Award 1 mark if both sentences have the correct words inserted. i Separate, different ii gardeners, sieves Do not give credit for only one sentence completed correctly.	1
	c.	Award 1 mark for an explanation along the following lines: Rest an empty sieve on top of a bucket or other suitable container. Sprinkle the mixture of fine soil and small pebbles carefully into the sieve and gently shake it. The small soil particles will fall through the mesh of the sieve into the bucket. The small pebbles will remain trapped in the sieve. The mixture of fine soil particles and small pebbles has been separated. Do not give credit for an explanation that does not include the use of a sieve.	1
6	a.	Award 1 mark if the arrowhead on line A and the arrowhead on line B are both correct. The arrowhead on line A should point to the eye. The arrowhead on line B should point to the mirror.	1

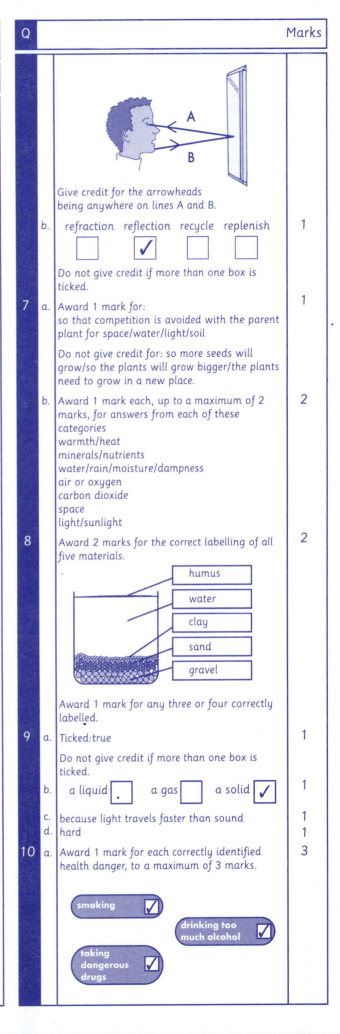

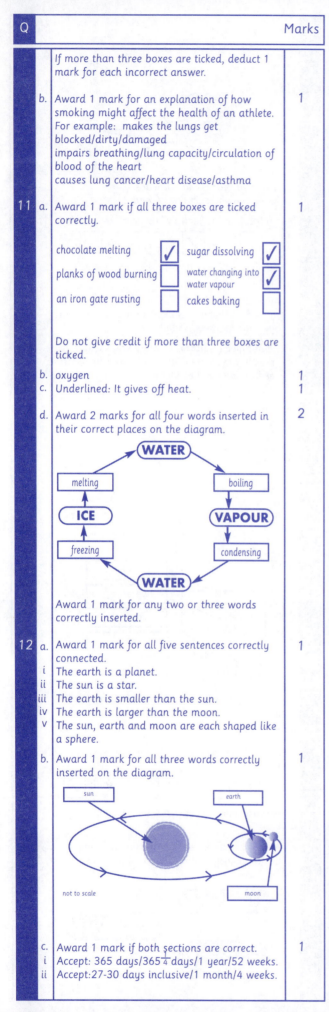

Pull-out instructions and answers

Working Out Your Child's National Curriculum Level

When working out your child's level from the information given on this page it must be remembered that the results obtained from the tests in this book are only a rough guide to your child's likely performance. They will, however, help to give your child valuable test practice and give you an insight into the strengths and weaknesses in their learning. Please remember, this has only been a practice test and the results obtained by your child should be interpreted as guidance only.

Once you have marked both tests enter the total number of marks scored by your child for each test in the appropriate box in the table below.

	TEST A	TEST B	TOTAL
Possible Total	50	50	100
Child's Mark			

Finding the level for Test A or Test B
You can convert your child's score for Test A or Test B into a National Curriculum level by comparing your child's mark against the level thresholds shown on the chart below.

Chart to Show Your Child's National Curriculum Level for Test A or Test B				
	Below Level 3	Level 3	Level 4	Level 5
Marks	0–8	9–25	26–41	42+

Finding the overall level for both tests.
Use the chart below and your child's total marks for the two tests to work out his or her overall level for science. **The target level for 10-11 year olds in Year 6 at Primary School is the upper half of the mark range for Level 4.** When interpreting your child's level, be aware that there is quite a wide range for each level. Check to see if your child has just gained a level, is in the middle of the mark range or has just missed a level by a mark or two.

Chart to Show Your Child's Overall National Curriculum Level				
	Below Level 3	Level 3	Level 4	Level 5
Marks	0–16	17–50	51–82	83+

Vocabulary Your Child Should Know

The word lists on the next page contain key vocabulary for science at Key Stage 2. Each list is made up of words that frequently occur in Key Stage 2 SATs. Learning the correct spelling and meaning of each word is important for the success of your child.
The words have been arranged in groups of ten for ease of learning. The two tick boxes after each word are there for you or your child to record progress. Put a tick in the first box when your child understands the scientific meaning of the word and a tick in the second box when your child can spell the word correctly. The word groups on the top half of the page are easier than those on the bottom half of the page.

vii   **Have a go! Science Tests   Ages 10–11**

Pull-out instructions and answers

Key Vocabulary
Easier words

warm-blooded		vibrate		fair test		stretch	
solid		melt		repel		sieve	
gravity		food chain		axis		incisor	
predict		freeze		milk teeth		anther	
petal		attract		soak		filter	
liquid		record		mixture		force	
stigma		pulse		molar		style	
gas		soluble		boil		mass	
stamen		muscle		push		prey	
steam		affect		result		absorb	

key		stem		reflect		brain	
shadow		volume		lungs		rotate	
mammal		seed		nectar		safe	
carpel		habitat		baby		explain	
oxygen		orbit		spin		process	
root		describe		diagram		weight	
leaf		skeleton		feature		heart	
pull		support		child		canine	
reason		pitch		adult		cold-blooded	
flower		idea		teenager		gram (g)	

Key Vocabulary
Harder words

producer		information		predator		mineral	
transparent		air resistance		material		condensation	
circuit		condense		magnetic force		absorbent	
investigate		consumer		pattern		pollination	
microbe		photosynthesis		increase		waterproof	
solution		water vapour		water cycle		magnetic	
evaporate		upthrust		diaphragm		property	
preserve		evidence		complete		seed dispersal	
friction		nutrient		organism		protection	
measure		reflection		conductor		permeable	

thermometer		non-magnetic		circulation		fertilisation	
newton (N)		combustion		flammable		dangerous	
germinate		nutrition		loudness		germination	
evaporation		movement		function		prediction	
forcemeter		dissolve		investigation		closed switch	
vibration		decrease		open switch		irreversible	
carbohydrate		experiment		reversible		symbol	
temperature		periscope		environment		luminous	
plaque		impermeable		translucent		flexible	
saturate		moisture		rotation		opaque	

Have a go! Science Tests Ages 10–11   viii

SCIENCE

KEY STAGE 2   LEVELS 3–5
TEST B

To do this test you will need a **pencil**, a **ruler**, a **rubber** and a **watch** or **clock** to time yourself.

Sit at a table in a quiet place.

Marking Grid

Page	Marks possible	Marks scored
18–19	6	
20–21	6	
22–23	8	
24–25	10	
26–27	5	
28–29	4	
30–31	7	
32	4	
Total	50	

Ask an adult to read through the test instructions with you before you start.

INSTRUCTIONS

1. You will have **45 minutes** to do this test.

2. Read all the words in each question carefully.

3. If you cannot read a word ask an adult to tell you what it says.

4. Use any diagrams or pictures to help you.

5. Try to explain your answers accurately if you are asked to do so.

6. Do not worry if you do not finish all the questions. Do as many as you can.

7. Do not waste time on a question you cannot do. Move quickly on to the next one.

8. Read instructions carefully and write your answers in the spaces highlighted by the handwriting symbols.

9. Move straight on from one page to the next without waiting to be told.

10. If there is time left when you have finished, check your answers and try to do any questions you missed out earlier.

Your first name	
Your last name	

Parents and teachers: Removable instructions and answers are in the centre of the book.

17

Teeth

1 This diagram shows the different teeth in your mouth.

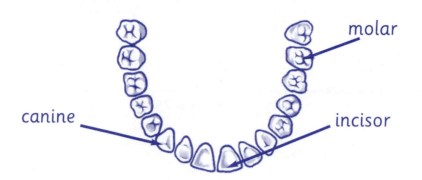

Different types of teeth do different jobs when we bite food.

a. What different jobs do these three types of teeth do?

i   incisor _____

ii molar _____

iii canine _____

Keeping your teeth healthy is very important.

b. Which of these things will help to keep your teeth healthy?

Tick TWO boxes.

eating less sugar ☐

drinking lots of water ☐

visiting the dentist regularly ☐

eating less fat ☐

Q1a

2 marks

Q1b

1 mark

Test B

Electrical conductors

2 Some children tested six materials to find out which material was an electrical conductor.
They set up the electrical circuit illustrated in the diagram.
The bulb lit up.
They then replaced wire A with different materials in turn.
The results they obtained are shown in the chart.

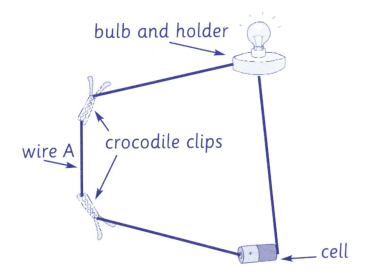

	bulb lights	bulb does not light
wool		✓
bronze	✓	
plastic		✓
wood		✓
copper	✓	
steel	✓	

a. Write the names of the materials that were good electrical conductors.

_____

b. What does it mean if the bulb does not light up?

_____

c. Write TRUE or FALSE after reading the statement below.

Most metals are good conductors of electricity.

_____

Test B

Shadows

3. John and Lucy carried out an experiment to discover how they could change the size of a shadow.
The diagram illustrates the apparatus they used.
Their results are shown on the graph.

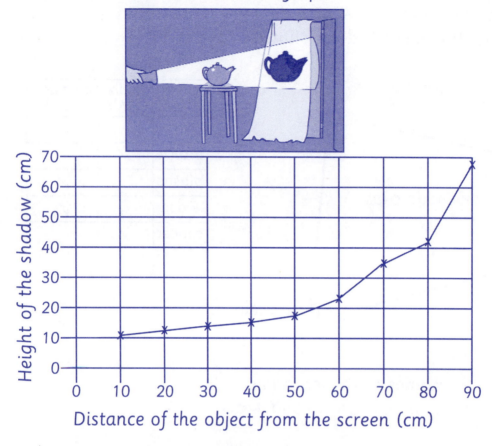

a. What height was the shadow when the object was 40cm from the screen? _____

b. When the height of the shadow was 35cm, how far was the object from the screen? _____

c. Choose the correct word to complete the sentence.

A shadow is formed when an _____ object blocks the light from a light source.

| opposite | open | offensive | opaque |

Identifying animals

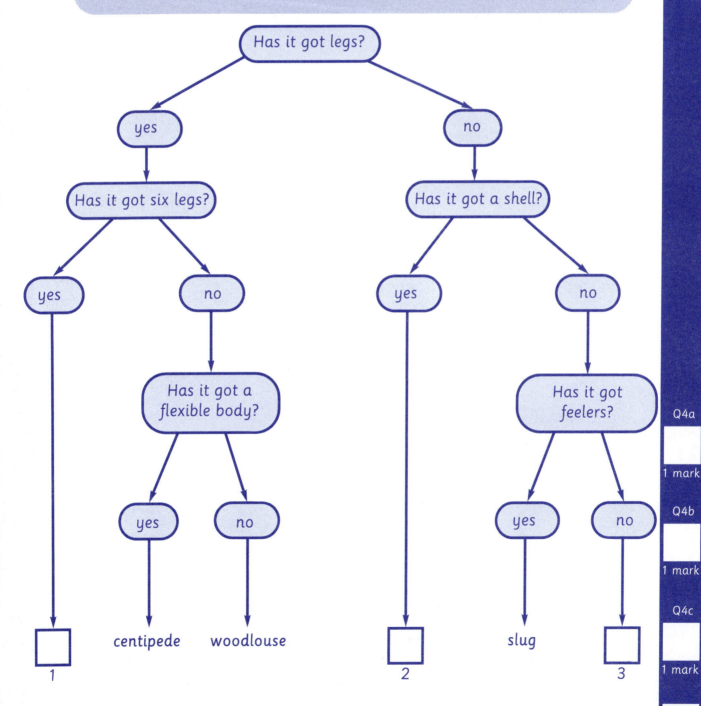

A snail **B** earthworm **C** beetle

These animals could be shown on this flowchart.
Write the correct letter in the correct box.

Test B

21

Total

Separating solids

5 **a.** Tick the sieve.

b. Complete these sentences by writing in the correct words from the box below.

i   A sieve will _____ a mixture of solids

of _____ sizes.

ii _____ can use _____ to

separate unwanted pebbles from soil.

| sieves | separate | gardeners | different |

c. Explain how you would separate a mixture of fine soil and small pebbles.

_____

_____

_____

_____

_____

Q5a

1 mark

Q5b

1 mark

Q5c

1 mark

Test B

22

Mirrors

6 Edward looks at his face in a mirror.

a. Draw an arrowhead on line A and B to show how the light travels.

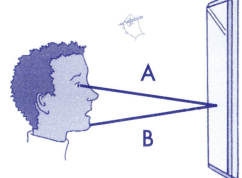

b. Tick the word that describes what happens to the light at the mirror.

refraction ☐   reflection ☐   recycle ☐   replenish ☐

Plant reproduction

7 a. Explain why it is important for seeds to be dispersed from the parent plant.

_____

_____

_____

b. Write TWO things that seeds need in order to germinate in the soil.

i _____

ii _____

Test B

23

Total

Soil

8 Some children mixed a sample of soil with water in a clear container. The drawing shows what the mixture looked like after a few days.

Choose the correct name to write in each box.

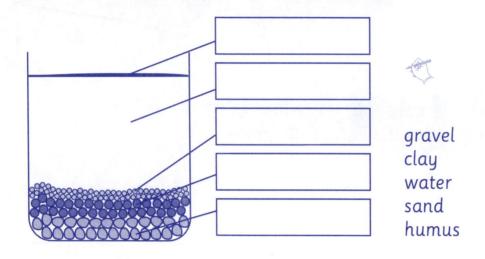

gravel
clay
water
sand
humus

Sound

9 a. Tick **true** or **false**.

Sound is only made when an object vibrates.

true ☐   false ☐

b. Through which type of material does sound travel fastest?

Tick **ONE** box.   a liquid ☐   a gas ☐   a solid ☐

c. Why do you **see** a distant car door close before you hear the slam?

_____

d. Use **ONE** word to complete this sentence.

To play a drum loudly you must hit it _____ .

Test B
24

Keeping healthy

 10 Some things people do are good for their health.
Some things people do can damage their health.
In extreme cases, doing these damaging things can even kill them.

a. Which of these things are dangerous to your health?

Tick **THREE** boxes.

- smoking ☐
- having enough rest ☐
- keeping yourself clean ☐
- drinking too much alcohol ☐
- taking dangerous drugs ☐
- good dental care ☐
- eating a balanced diet ☐
- taking exercise ☐

b. How might smoking make athletes less fit and healthy?

_____

_____

Test B

Q10a 3 marks

Q10b 1 mark

Total

Changing materials

 11. Some changes to materials can be reversed.
This means that the material can be changed back to how it was.
A change of this kind is called a **reversible** change.

Some changes to materials cannot be reversed.
This means that the material cannot be changed back to how it was.
A change of this kind is called an **irreversible** change.

a. Which of these changes are reversible?

Tick **THREE** boxes.

chocolate melting ☐

planks of wood burning ☐

an iron gate rusting ☐

sugar dissolving ☐

water changing into water vapour ☐

cakes baking ☐

Burning changes materials.

b. Write the name of the gas on which burning depends.

_____

Test B

26

c. When plaster of Paris hardens, an irreversible change takes place.

What happens to plaster of Paris as it hardens?

Underline the correct answer.

It changes colour.

It crumbles into a powder.

It gives off heat.

d. Add the missing words to this flow chart diagram. Choose from the words at the bottom of the page.

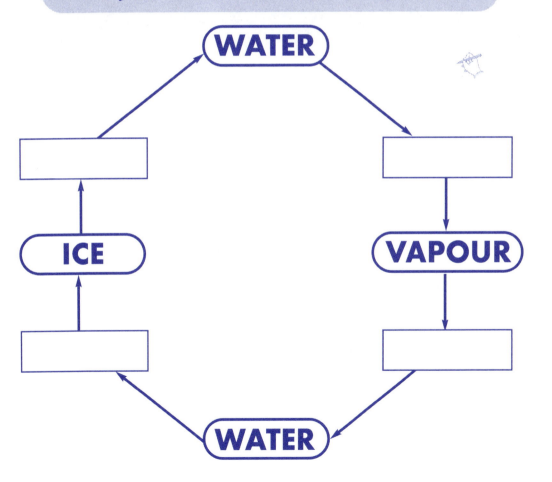

condensing   melting   boiling   freezing

The earth and beyond

12

a. Connect the start of each sentence to its most suitable ending.

Starts	Endings
i The earth is a	star.
ii The sun is a	moon.
iii The earth is smaller than the	planet.
iv The earth is larger than the	sphere.
v The sun, earth and moon are each shaped like a	sun.

Q12a

1 mark

Test B

b. Write **sun**, **earth** and **moon** in the correct boxes on the diagram.

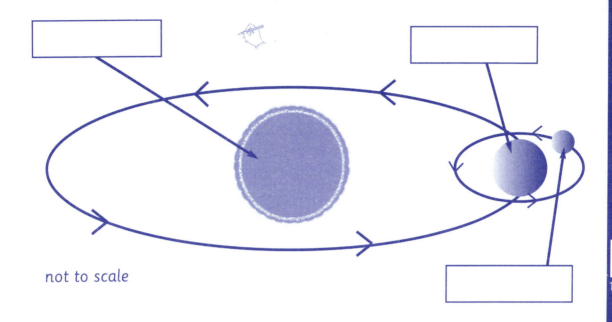

not to scale

c. Answer these questions.

i How long does it take the earth to orbit the sun?

ii How long does it take the moon to orbit the earth?

_____

d. This diagram shows the axis on which the earth rotates.

the earth

axis

Draw a line on the diagram to mark the equator.

Test B   29   Total

Feeding relationships

13 Complete these food chains involving the plant and the animals above each one.

a.

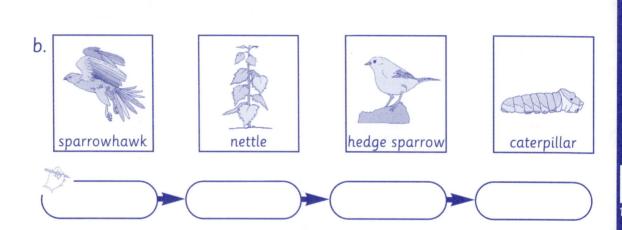

| perch | tadpole | pondweed | stickleback |

b.

| sparrowhawk | nettle | hedge sparrow | caterpillar |

c. Complete these sentences using the plant and the animals from part a above.

i   The consumer that is not a predator is the _____ .

ii The _____ is a predator and also a prey.

iii The producer in the food chain is the _____ .

iv The _____ is a predator but not a prey.

Burning

14 Nasreen holds different materials in tongs over the flame of a candle.
She watches carefully to see what happens to each material.
She records her observations on a piece of paper.

The table shows her findings.

Material	Observations
cotton	Flames appear quickly. Grey ash left.
chocolate	Bubbles, smokes and then turns black
pebble	Black coating. Nothing else happens.
wax	Went runny followed by flames and smoke.
cardboard	Flames. Brittle black material left over.
steel nail	Black coating. Nothing else happens.

a. Which **TWO** materials melted and then burned?

_____

Q14a

1 mark

b. What will happen to a wooden lollipop stick if Nasreen holds it in her tongs over the flame?

_____

Q14b

1 mark

c. Ring the word below that means the same as burning.

compatible   circulation   combustion   condensation

Q14c

1 mark

Test B

31

Total

Magnets

15 a. Label the poles of each magnet by writing N or S in the correct places. The magnets are **attracting** each other.

 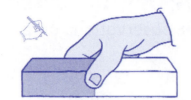

b. Why did you choose to label the magnets in the way you did?

_____

_____

c. Label the poles of each magnet by writing N or S in the correct places. The magnets are **repelling** each other.

d. Why did you choose to label the magnets in the way you did?

_____

_____

STOP HERE

Test B